What You Need to Know about

Japanese Knotweed

A UK guide for the non-specialist

Jim Glaister

PACKARD PUBLISHING LIMITED
CHICHESTER

What You Need to Know about Japanese Knotweed
© James Lloyd Glaister 2022

First published in 2022 by Packard Publishing Limited, 14 Guilden Road, Chichester, West Sussex, PO19 7LA, UK.

ISBN 978-1-85341-168-7

A CIP catalogue record of this book is available from the British Library.

Picture credits: Paul Copper (Figs. 4.2, 4.3 (part), 5.6, 7 & 16, Kevin Gilderson (4.4 part), Brian Taylor (1.2); all others by the Author.

Prepared for Press by Michael Packard

Layout and design by Hilite Design, Marchwood, Southampton, Hampshire, SO40 4UL.

Printed and bound in the UK by Lemonade Print Group Ltd, Burgess Hill, West Sussex, RH15 8QY.

Contents

A note to readers

This book has been written in the United Kingdom and therefore has a British bias. The specifics of the law and the attitudes of bodies, such as mortgage lenders, focus on the United Kingdom.

Japanese knotweed is the most commonly found species of knotweed, but it should be recognised that other problematic forms found in the UK are giant, dwarf and Himalayan knotweeds, and various forms of hybrid knotweed, the most common being 'bohemica'.

In the interests of clarity, it should be assumed that any references to 'Japanese knotweed' or 'knotweed' throughout this book include those other species, unless otherwise stated.

There are widely adopted rules, created by Linnaeus in 1753, for the written presentation of scientific Latin names of all species, whereby the genus (e.g. *Reynoutria*) comes first and is capitalised, followed by the species (e.g. *japonica*) which isn't. However, common names, which are colloquial and non-scientific, are less formalised and there are no international conventions on how they can be written – hence the reader will find references in different sources to Japanese Knotweed and Japanese knotweed.

Publishers generally use lower case letters for all common names, though some prefer capitalising each word for the purposes of clarity to ensure the reader won't confuse which words in a sentence are part of the name. This book will follow the standard publishing model, as the author believes 'knotweed' is not a word that can be misinterpreted within a sentence.

This pocket edition provides the essential information about dealing with knotweed for the benefit of the general public and as a primer for other professional people, such as estate agents, land managers and solicitors. If readers require more detailed historical, legal or general background to the points made below, they may care to check the Author's *Japanese Knotweed Management in the UK – a Practical Guide for Invasive Weed Practitioners*, or his various factsheets from www.jkweed.co.uk.

Figure 1.1 *When a residential garden consists almost entirely of Japanese knotweed, it's a good indication of both neglect and denial (see page 1).*

1. Introduction

Japanese knotweed has become something of a media phenomenon. At the turn of the twenty-first century, most members of the public in the UK had never heard of it. Those in the know grew increasingly concerned about how prevalent knotweed had become and the danger it presented to the environment. In 2006, the Environment Agency placed Japanese knotweed at the top of its list of 'Top Ten Unwanted Species in Britain'.

While the first decade of the century progressed, attitudes to knotweed evolved from horror stories told in pubs to major articles in newspapers or comments on television. Japanese knotweed became a by-word for anything deemed to be bad.

Public attitudes

There are three things a majority of the general public believes to be true about knotweed on their properties:

1. Their house will be destroyed by the knotweed;
2. They will never be able to use their garden again because knotweed cannot be killed;
3. They will never be able to sell their house.

The real situation is not as dire as these fears would project, but none of these beliefs is helpful, and can often result in the knotweed issue becoming much more difficult to handle. Nevertheless, there are two prevalent reactions among members of the public: denial or panic.

With denial, people just ignore the knotweed and hope it will go away. Consequently, the plant continues to spread and, if neglected for long enough, will come to completely dominate the location where it is growing (Figure 1.1). If this location is a standard residential garden, it will almost invariably spread into surrounding properties as well. The larger the infestation – and particularly the more properties that are involved – the more complicated and expensive the programme of treatment will end up being.

With panic, people tend either to come up with their own, often brutal, solutions or simply try to hide the existence of the knotweed (Figure 1.2). Their reactions can vary, but can include pulling up knotweed material, partially digging out the plant, setting fire to it, over-treating it with herbicide, throwing diesel or some other environmentally damaging product on it, covering it with membrane or concrete, or continually cutting and mowing it. None of these measures provides a long-term solution and, in most cases, they simply spread the knotweed to other areas.

Figure 1.2 *Prior to a survey, a householder selling their property removed knotweed material from the garden and placed it in the recycling bins. The green bin contained a viable knotweed crown, and the blue one some rhizome and stems.*

Knotweed is invasive and can establish itself almost anywhere (Figure 1.3), often from the tiniest fragments of itself, but dealing with it can be easier than you think. All it takes is a sensible, methodical approach, though lasting treatment is rarely a 'quick fix': it typically takes several years to achieve a full and permanent solution.

Unless you really know what you are doing, and have access to the right equipment and materials, it is best to leave management of knotweed to professionals. Whatever you choose to do, it is important to identify the plant and its component parts, and to understand its life-cycle in order that it can be effectively treated and controlled.

Figure 1.3 Knotweed has found a way to grow in an apparently built-up location.

2. Recognise your plant

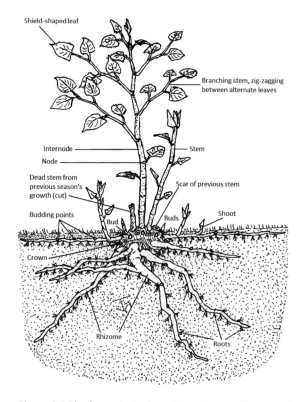

Figure 2.1 *The four principal constituent parts of knotweed are the stems, leaves, crowns and rhizomes. The stems and leaves are the feeding organs of the plant, absorbing moisture and energy which are then transferred to other parts. The crown provides stability and functions as a storage organ. The rhizomes are foraging organs, seeking nutrients in the soil and pushing further afield to find new sources. During the winter, the rhizome reverts to being a storage organ.*

Japanese knotweed is an herbaceous plant, often described as a rhizomatous perennial; that is, each plant lives for many years and spreads by means of its rhizome (or underground stem) system to dominate any area where it establishes itself. It currently occupies most regions of the UK and Ireland, except Orkney and some other offshore islands. Its botanical name is now fixed as *Reynoutria japonica,* though it was previously known as *Fallopia japonica.*

Figure 2.2 *The visible part of knotweed consists of bamboo-like, hollow, jointed stems, with alternate, shield-shaped mid-green leaves. The joints in the stems are known as nodes, with the stretches of stem between the nodes termed internodes. Stems can reach diameters of up to 40 mm.*

Figure 2.3 *Clusters of small creamy-white flowers adorn the plant from August until around October or November, arising from the angle formed between the stem and the leaf. All of this visible material dies back following the first harsh frost of the year, leaving only dead, erect, brown, brittle canes throughout the winter. These often remain in situ for two to three years. Fresh winter canes will retain a degree of orangey-red colouring, gradually reverting to a pale brown over the subsequent two to three years.*

Figure 2.4 New shoots appear in early spring, initially reminiscent in appearance of asparagus spears in mature plants. The shoots are crimson in colour, including the rolled-up leaves. The leaves unfurl within a few days of appearing, gradually turning green as they mature. Knotweed grows quickly to an average height of 2 to 3 m by the summer; once it has gained its full height, it will stabilise for the rest of the season.

Figure 2.5 *Beneath the ground lies the secret of knotweed's ability to colonise large areas. The crowns, which form in more mature plants, are extremely long-lived, and it is from these that the aerial stems and subterranean rhizomes grow. Crowns consist of very dense material. In mature plants they can be huge and are typically found partially above the surface of the ground and can survive drying out and even burning if they are not subjected to high enough temperatures for a long enough period of time. Fragments of live crown material can produce new growth wherever they are deposited.*

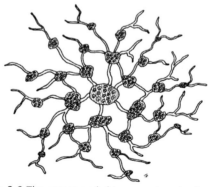

Figure 2.6 *The crown and rhizome network of a mature knotweed stand, as viewed from above, with the larger crowns being the oldest. This illustration has been simplified and shows a uniformity of spread that is rarely replicated in nature.*

Figure 2.7 *Rhizomes vary in diameter, typically from 5 to 100 mm, and can usually extend up to 2 m from the parent plant for small infestations, or up to 4 m for well-established stands. Rhizomes rarely reach depths beyond 2 m. They have a distinctive orange colour internally, though young rhizomes tend to be white. Fibrous roots grow from the crowns and rhizomes.*

Knotweed's subterranean system survives the winter by storing nutrients (sucrose) drawn down to the crowns and rhizomes from the stems and leaves. This process, usually referred to as the 'senescence' period, is triggered by the first frosts. The leaves turn yellow and drop, and the plant will shut down by inducing temporary dormancy, enabling it to survive through the winter. The crowns and rhizomes use the nutrients they have stored over the winter months to 'kick start' the spring 'rebirth', resulting in the vigorous spring growth.

How does it reproduce?

- Plants in the UK originated from cuttings taken from a single specimen imported during the 19th century; consequently, they are all female.

- In the UK, Japanese knotweed is not pollinated by male plants due to their absence, but if seeds are found they are rarely viable. Japanese knotweed can hybridise with other knotweed species where male plants are present.

- Knotweed can reproduce vegetatively through the regeneration of fragments of itself.
- Crowns and rhizomes are highly regenerative; 0.7 g (about the size of a fingernail) is capable of producing new growth.
- Stems in water transported by flooding have been found to produce new growth within 6 days (probably with a small amount of crown or rhizome material attached).
- Knotweed is capable of growing in a wide range of locations, soil types and pH levels.

How has it become so widespread?

- Japanese knotweed is native to parts of China, Sakhalin Island, the Kurile Islands, Korea, Vietnam, Taiwan, and of course Japan.
- It was 'discovered' in the 18th and early 19th centuries by botanists in Japan working for the Dutch army and brought to Europe, where it was propagated and spread from Holland by nurserymen.
- In the UK, it was widely promoted in the late 19th and early 20th centuries as an ornamental plant and grown in some of the most fashionable gardens in the country.
- For about 87 years it was enthusiastically bought, sold and grown from cuttings.
- Human activity is a primary force behind knotweed becoming so widely established; it has been mulched, chipped, fly-tipped, generally transported and deposited illegally.
- Transport vehicles, such as trains, cars, lorries and boats, can pick up knotweed fragments and deposit them a few miles further along as they travel.

The 20th century saw increasing awareness of the dangers of allowing knotweed to establish itself in the UK. It could be openly purchased during the 1930s and even up to 1990, but it wasn't until The Wildlife and Countryside Act of 1981 and later the Environmental Protection Act 1991 that a legal infrastructure was introduced to dictate where knotweed could be planted and how it should be disposed of.

Different forms of knotweed and other similar plants

There are some other knotweed species commonly found in the UK: giant (*Reynoutria sachalinensis*), Himalayan (*Persicaria wallichii*), dwarf Japanese (*Reynoutria japonica* var. 'Compacta'), lesser (*Persicaria campanulata*) and hybrids, such as 'Bohemica' and *Fallopia* x *conollyana*.

The treatment of these varieties is the same as for Japanese knotweed, and their identification can be made by specialist contractors. There are other totally different plants which are commonly mistaken for knotweed, such as bindweed, broad-leaved dock, cornus (dogwood), Himalayan balsam, Himalayan honeysuckle, *Houttuynia cordata,* lilac, ivy, pale persicaria, poplar suckers and Russian vine. These species show similarities in leaf-shapes, stem colouring or growing habits, but if you are in doubt, most contractors will offer a free identification service that allows photographs of a suspect plant to be e-mailed to them. Provided the images submitted are clear enough, one e-mail can be all that is required to confirm whether a plant is knotweed or not.

3. Dealing with knotweed on properties

Anything you or someone you instruct does that will spread knotweed material to other areas will end up making life difficult for you. As a simple guide to what to do and not do, use the tables below:

DON'T	Flail or strim knotweed, as this will cause the knotweed to spread.
DON'T	Cut down or pull green knotweed growth, as this material is still viable. Pulling knotweed will initially encourage further growth, and is likely to pull up the highly regenerative crowns creating a disposal problem.
DON'T	Use standard garden waste or a local amenity tip to dispose of any viable knotweed material, as this will encourage knotweed spread and put you in breach of the law. Do not fly-tip knotweed material.
DON'T	Conduct any home efforts at treatment without sufficient knowledge, as your attempts could make the situation worse in the long term, and could invalidate any subsequent professional treatment.
DON'T	Cover the knotweed area, as any suppression will only be temporary and could impede any subsequent treatment.
DON'T	Chip knotweed material, as mechanical chippers do not kill the plant and could result in new knotweed growth wherever the chipped material is spread.

DON'T	Add Japanese knotweed to compost, as this can lead to knotweed growing in the compost heap.
DON'T	Allow knotweed to spread into adjacent properties, as this could result in some form of legal action by your neighbour(s).
DON'T	Break the law – knotweed material and soil containing knotweed material is classed as a controlled waste and must be disposed of accordingly.

DO	Inspect your site (or have your property inspected) for the presence of knotweed before you commence any works whatsoever. This includes landscaping or building extensions.
DO	Be aware of your legal responsibilities of knotweed disposal. If off-site disposal is necessary, ensure it is sent to a licensed landfill facility accompanied by the appropriate waste transfer documentation.
DO	Treat knotweed as soon as it becomes apparent (but at the correct time of year) – do not allow it to become established or spread.
DO	Prevent any disturbance of the plant, particularly during the growing season, and prevent disturbance of the ground within up to seven metres – or at least two to four metres – of the plant at any time of the year.
DO	Consult a suitably qualified/experienced Japanese knotweed specialist if in doubt. See Chapter 5 for information on finding advice.

What should you do if knotweed is growing in your garden?

The best advice is: don't ignore it. It is in knotweed's nature to spread. In time the rhizomes will encroach into the surrounding area, so don't let your garden become like the one pictured in Figure 3.1.

Dealing with knotweed should not be driven by panic. Keep a cool head and follow these easy steps:

1. Make sure it is knotweed – most knotweed contractors offer free identification, which they will confirm from emailed photographs (it is always better to send two images; a close up of the stem and leaf, and a wider shot of the entire plant).

2. Most knotweed contractors will offer a paid verification service, entailing a site visit and the production of a brief report on whether the plant in question is knotweed or not.

3. Is the infestation also next door? Communication with your neighbours is key, and avoid angry or provocative language in discussions.

4. Do you need a knotweed survey? A mortgage lender will probably insist on one prepared by a suitable specialist; a purchaser or lender may require an insurance-backed guarantee (IBG – see below, p 47).

5. Are you planning to re-landscape the garden, extend the house, or build a conservatory or outbuilding in the vicinity of the knotweed area? If not, and the area is to remain undisturbed for the foreseeable future, you can implement a treatment programme.

6. Commence a herbicide treatment programme. This will help control the infestation, but will not eradicate the plant, so be aware of the following:
   a) Follow the dosage instructions meticulously;
   b) Apply the herbicide at the right time of the year;
   c) A management plan is essential;
   d) Include neighbouring knotweed in the programme.

7. Leave the area undisturbed.

Summary:

- Do not ignore the knotweed.
- Do not try to tackle it yourself unless you know exactly what you are doing.
- Seek the co-operation of your neighbours to avoid any unpleasant future conflict.
- Remember, it is in your own interest not to take an indifferent attitude to the plant.
- Ensure you do not allow the situation to get out of control.

Figure 3.1 Knotweed spreading across several boundaries to affect four adjoining properties.

What legal recourse do you have if it spreads onto your land?

The responsibility for the control of knotweed rests with a houseowner, or manager of the land on which it is growing.

- The Environment Agencies (EA, NRW, SEPA, NIEA – see Glossary) are only concerned about knotweed if it is incorrectly disposed of, or if it has been treated with herbicide that has led to the contamination of watercourses or the water supply.

- Disputes between neighbours resulting from knotweed spreading across boundaries are largely a civil matter and expensive third-party litigation is often the only legal option available.
- In a dispute, always try to reach an amicable and informal agreement with your neighbour.
- If relations completely break down, and persistent problems remain, there are few options open other than involving your local authority.
- Councils which prosecute will be guided by the relevant sections of the Anti-Social Behaviour, Crime and Policing Act 2014, but interpretations may vary from council to council.
- Those afflicted by their neighbours' knotweed can seek private prosecutions in the Civil Court. Many of these cases have become more frequent, but often settle or collapse before they reach court, since they can prove to be expensive in solicitors' fees, etc.
- A legal precedent was created by the ruling in the High Court against Network Rail in 2018 that sided against landowners who failed to control knotweed on their land and allowed it to escape the confines of their boundaries.

Figure 3.2 A site that has been surface-scraped.

Buying property with knotweed growing on it

Some unscrupulous property owners will attempt to hide the knotweed present on the property they are selling. If you are looking to purchase land, look out for certain warning signs:

- Be wary if the ground looks freshly scraped (Fig. 3.2) or turned over; ask questions as the landowner may be trying to hide something;
- If there is evidence of recent landscaping in a garden, or if part of a shrub bed is covered, there may be undeclared knotweed in them;
- Have a quick look in the garden waste bin or in any garden refuse sacks lying around; if you find any cut knotweed stems or pieces of crown or rhizome, start asking questions; (Fig .3.3)
- Be careful about purchasing property during the winter; it can be virtually impossible to spot knotweed unless the crowns are prominent or mature stems are uncut.

Figure 3.3 *Cut knotweed stems and hastily dug up crowns and rhizomes are a good indication that someone is trying to hide their knotweed.*

17

If the knotweed is evident on the site and the owner is open about it, things are much more straightforward. You should be able to learn:

- Whether a management plan is in place;
- About previous treatments and whether a glyphosate-based herbicide was used;
- Whether the knotweed has been previously disturbed in any way, so the extent of the infestation can be identified.

These are all important facts when calculating how much cost will be involved, and if you need to deal with the knotweed problem after you buy the land or property. Thus:

- Obtain a quotation from a knotweed specialist (or several specialists) to obtain a figure you can take into negotiations.
- A seller is more likely to agree to your offer if you can back it with authoritative figures for the cost of getting rid of their knotweed.

Mortgage lenders and the property market

During the period 2008-2013 it was extremely difficult to obtain a mortgage if knotweed was present on or next to a property. Many believe that still to be the case, though the situation has been much more relaxed since 2013/14. Most of the big High Street lenders have been prepared in principle to lend on properties provided:

- There is a treatment or remediation plan in place;
- It is being executed by a member of a recognised trade body;
- There are appropriate guarantees and insurance in place.

Since the end of 2021, sky-rocketing house prices and increasing bank base-rates have complicated the situation, so that lenders now tend to require larger deposits from prospective house-buyers.

Lending decisions concerning knotweed-affected properties have been led since 2012 by guidance from the Royal Institution of Chartered Surveyors (RICS). New guidance from RICS came into effect on the 23rd March 2022, with the primary objective of providing objectivity and consistency in the advice surveyors and valuers present to mortgage lenders. The emphasis on distance (the 7m rule) has been discarded in favour of assessing the impact the knotweed is likely to have on structures and amenity use. The knotweed is categorised as to whether it requires action, management or reporting and the guidance makes it clear that 'ignoring Japanese knotweed is not an acceptable strategy'. As such, the requirements listed in the bullet points above still stand.

Since 2013, knotweed has featured as part of The Law Society's TA6 Property Information Form in England and Wales.

- All vendors in England and Wales are obliged to complete this form when selling their property and to sign a copy.
- The TA6 requires vendors to declare the current or historic presence of knotweed.
- If knotweed is/has been present, vendors are required to provide a copy of the knotweed management plan, along with any insurance cover linked to it.
- The TA6 is a legal document requiring notification of the presence of Japanese knotweed; fraudulent misrepresentation is dealt with severely by the law.

At the time of writing (February 2022), the Property Questionnaire as part of the Home Report used in Scotland and the 'Replies to Pre-contract Enquiries form' published by the Law Society of Northern Ireland do not contain any questions specific to Japanese knotweed.

4. Why is Japanese knotweed a cause for concern?

Environmental impact

Any species taken from its natural habitat and introduced into a different part of the world can have an impact on its new surroundings. In Asia, knotweed is kept in check by natural means. In the UK and Ireland, there are no natural predators and the plant is thriving, often at the expense of many less competitive native species.

Figure 4.1 *The thick concentration of stems and the tall leaf canopy in a mature Japanese knotweed stand (left). The dense canopy and accumulating leaf debris (right) reduces light within a knotweed stand, making it difficult for other plants to grow and compete.*

- Many UK native plants are 'shaded out' by knotweed's spreading growth and thick leaf-canopy.
- Its leaf-fall in late autumn produces a dense mulch on the ground, allowing little to grow through it.
- It reduces the natural biodiversity of plant life and can have an extremely negative effect on any rare plants close by.
- It restricts access to rivers and increases the risk of flooding.
- Further infestations of knotweed can occur downstream if stems attached to crown or rhizomatous material are washed away or scoured from river banks by flood water.
- Mature stands can retain non-biodegradable rubbish and litter.

Figure 4.2 *Litter accumulating in a Japanese knotweed stand.*

Structural damage

Japanese knotweed has a well-established, but over-exaggerated, reputation amongst the public as a destroyer of the built environment, damaging paving, tarmac, concrete surfaces, walls, building foundations, flood defences, drainage systems and archaeological sites.

Figure 4.3 *Knotweed will find its way through weaknesses in walls (right) and will exacerbate weaknesses as they grow (top-left). It will readily grow through the gaps between paving (centre top and bottom) and can, in the right circumstances, grow through tarmac (bottom-left).*

- Knotweed exploits weaknesses, but is unlikely to cause them. If there is a void, crack or hole in a wall, knotweed shoots can explore them and eventually increase the size of the fissure as it grows.

- If tarmac is soft (freshly laid) or is decaying, knotweed can push through to the surface, increasing the level of damage as it grows and spreads.
- If concrete is thin, cracked or otherwise in poor condition, knotweed can find a way to the surface and heighten the level of destruction.

But if all of these surfaces are in a good state of repair, knotweed is unlikely to do much damage. The biggest myth that surrounds knotweed is that it can grow through building foundations and level the structure to the ground. This is not true. If knotweed is discovered to damage a building's foundation, it is because the footings were already in poor condition, and the knotweed has simply taken advantage of an existing fault and made it worse.

The kind of damage most typically caused by knotweed is to:

- Paving, where the knotweed emerges around the edges of the slabs and pushes them out of alignment;
- Concrete or tarmac, where the surface is already decaying, freshly laid or incorrectly laid;
- Drains, where the knotweed rhizomes can run and can take advantage of the moisture caused by cracked pipes;
- Single-skin walls, where fault lines are more likely to pass through the full width of the wall, allowing the knotweed to exacerbate them, or where knotweed maturity can unbalance the base of the wall;
- Cavity walls, where the knotweed has a route of access into the cavity.

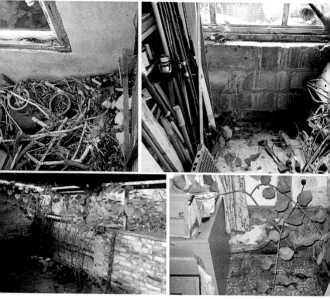

Figure 4.4 *It is common to find knotweed emerging within sheds (top) or outbuildings (bottom-left) due to weaknesses in the floors. Knotweed emerging within a house (bottom-right) is rare and only occurs if there is an access route, such as a hole in a wall, service duct, etc.*

Knotweed is more likely to have a detrimental effect on boundary walls and outbuildings than habitable residential and commercial premises. A well-constructed wall in a good state of repair is far less likely to be penetrated. However, if knotweed rhizomes find a service duct, ventilation grille or another similar means of accessing a building, it may explore it. Photographs of knotweed growing inside buildings usually show the result of this type of encroachment.

Figure 4.5 *Building walls or laying concrete over mature knotweed rarely works out well. Either immediately, or after a period of dormancy, the knotweed will typically find a route around the edges, through expansion gaps or via some other inherent weakness in the construction.*

There are two very specific circumstances when knotweed is sure to have a marked detrimental effect on the built environment, though both are the result of either ignorance, incompetence or neglect.

1. When a structure is built directly on top of an established knotweed stand without the knotweed being properly removed beforehand. This can range from a householder laying a patio or path over the area to a builder erecting a conservatory, house extension, commercial unit or full housing development on top of the knotweed. Fortunately, most professional developers and builders are now sufficiently aware of knotweed not to make this rudimentary mistake. However, instances do still occur.

Figure 4.6 Knotweed has been allowed to establish between an outbuilding and a boundary wall. After many years of growth and spread, the knotweed crowns and rhizomes are pushing the wall over. Six months later, the wall is gone.

2. Neglect. If knotweed is left to thrive for a few years it will form crowns. These crowns are dense and woody, providing a fairly solid surface with which to exert gradual force on a wall, paving slab, concrete, etc. If the crown is growing adjacent to the base of a boundary wall, it can start to push the wall over. If the crown is left to enlarge over time in a restricted space, the situation can become much more serious, as the crown will exert forces against the structures hemming it in. If a structure has inherent weaknesses, or if the crown is growing between two structures of unequal rigidity, major damage can result.

Is Japanese knotweed a health risk?

The answer is no.

- Knotweed tastes like rhubarb when cooked, is high in Vitamin C and large quantities will act as a mild laxative.
- Its rhizome is a rich source of resveratrol, a naturally-occurring anti-bacterial and anti-fungal chemical produced by plants to stave off disease.
- Commercially manufactured resveratrol is sold worldwide as a nutritional supplement and in the treatment of a wide range of allergic and inflammatory complaints.

5. Methods of treatment – what the professionals can do for you

It is important to realize that there is no quick solution for the control of Japanese knotweed.

Lois Child & Max Wade, *The Japanese Knotweed Manual*

Essentially, there are two methods of dealing with knotweed: either you dig it up, or you leave it where it is and treat it with a herbicide. Between these two extremes there are a number of methods in common practice, so knotweed management will typically be carried out by using one or a combination of the following:

- Herbicidal treatment programme;
- Excavation and disposal off-site;
- Excavation and burial on site;
- Excavation and relocation on site (bunding);
- Reduced excavation and capping with a root barrier.

Unless you have the knowledge, equipment and space to carry out the tasks mentioned above, it is best to leave the programme to a knotweed specialist. Even then, choose a professional wisely (see below) and be wary of advice provided on the Internet. Beware of the quick fix!

The key to successful knotweed management is to understand the plant's growing cycle and its natural tendency towards dormancy; treatments and methodologies can then be optimised. Procedures and terms used are mentioned below.

Control or eradication

The word 'eradication' is an over-used and imprecise term which is now actively discouraged by organisations such as the Property Care Association. Its use can unfortunately be found in many specifications drawn up by developers, ecologists and local authorities. Most remedial methods are used to achieve control, not eradication. It is a critical distinction, as there may be long-term considerations involved when methods of control have been used.

'Eradication' of Japanese knotweed refers to its complete removal, which can only occur if the plant is fully excavated and disposed of. For many residential and commercial properties, such an operation would be prohibitively expensive and often impractical. It may also be impossible to remove all of the knotweed if any of it has crossed a property's boundary.

Control by herbicide

A herbicidal treatment programme can provide a very effective way of dealing with knotweed on residential properties, whether conducted by a suitably knowledgeable homeowner or by a professional contractor, but remember:

- It is a means of control; full eradication cannot be guaranteed; it can kill most of the plant and leave any viable rhizomes lacking enough energy to produce new growth;
- If left undisturbed, the remainder will become dormant and eventually die;
- If the viable rhizome is severed from the adjoining dead part, new growth could be generated.
- Herbicidal control takes years to complete, but is the most economic remedy to take;
- Herbicide treatments are only effective if applied at the optimum time of the year and at the recommended dose rates;
- If future building works or re-landscaping occur in the knotweed area, other methods are likely to be needed.

For a typical residential property, a herbicidal-treatment programme will be the most commonly used form of remediation.

Figure 5.1 *Foliar application of herbicide to knotweed leaves.*

Glyphosate

The most commonly used herbicide contains glyphosate as its active ingredient. 'Roundup' is the most well-known brand name, which can be purchased off the shelf at garden centres, including in pre-diluted, 'ready to use' spraying forms.

Glyphosate is what is called a 'translocating' herbicide, meaning it is absorbed by the plant and moves (or translocates) within the plant down to the roots. Knotweeds transport nutrients, such as sucrose, from their foliage down to the roots in order to provide energy to increase their growth. Once applied to the leaves – known as foliar application (Figure 5.1) – the glyphosate will be moved within the plant as part of this process, effectively killing the plant from the inside.

- The best time to apply a glyphosate herbicide is between flowering and leaf drop. This is typically between August and October in the UK after the surface growth has reached its optimum height for that season.
- It can take between 14 to 28 days before the effects of a single application become evident on the visible part of a plant.
- If a plant is large and has a substantial root or rhizome system, the full effects may not be apparent on the top growth until the following growing season.
- Leaves turning brown and dropping off a few days after an application indicate that the treatment has not been particularly successful.
- If the leaves are burned off quickly, it is probable that very little of the herbicide was absorbed and translocated to the rhizomes.
- Glyphosate is 'non-residual', which means it does not act on the soil and will not leach to affect the roots of other shrubs and trees in close proximity to the target plant.
- Glyphosate is non-selective. It will also kill any grass, trees or shrubs (particularly immature ones) with which it comes into direct contact; accurate application is crucial.
- Glyphosate is only effective when applied to fresh leaves and green shoots.

For advice on the best choice of herbicide for your own site you should always contact a qualified BASIS Advisor (see Glossary). A stockist or supplier of herbicides or other pesticides (including supermarkets) is required when asked to put you in touch with a suitably qualified person before you make your purchase.

- A typical control programme for knotweed using glyphosate can take at least 3 to 4 years of treatments, followed by some post-treatment monitoring, to complete.
- Some knotweed infestations may need to be treated for 5 or 6 years; for large mature stands, 10-year programmes are not uncommon.

- If knotweed is growing in nutrient-rich soil, such as beside a watercourse, expect to extend the treatment programme by a few years.
- Conversely, if the knotweed is newly arrived and immature, it may be killed off within a couple of years.
- It is advisable to cut down the dead stems during the first winter of a treatment programme, particularly on larger knotweed stands (Figure 5.2).
- Post-treatment monitoring is crucial for a successful completion of the programme to be reached.
- The purpose of the monitoring is to inspect the knotweed area during the active growing season for any new growth.
- The propensity of knotweed to retreat into dormancy when put under stress means new growth can emerge several years after treatment seems to have been completed.
- Post-treatment monitoring should take place for several years with 2 years as an absolute minimum.

There are several methods of applying herbicide to knotweed.

- The most effective is to use either a hand-held or a knapsack sprayer (Figure 5.3).
- On smaller knotweed plants, the herbicide can be applied with a paintbrush, sponge or special applicator (known as 'weed wiping').
- Stem injection, whereby the herbicide is injected via a needle directly into the stem of the plant however, it is very easy to overdose, which in turn can lead to dormancy – see below.
- The so-called 'cut and fill' method, whereby living knotweed stems are cut down and herbicide is injected directly into the top of the cut stump. It is debatable how much more effective this method is and is it certainly unlikely to be effective if conducted outside the period of senescence.

Figure 5.2 Dead knotweed stems of a large, mature stand that have been cut during the winter.

Figure 5.3 Using a knapsack sprayer to apply herbicide to knotweed.

The healthier the knotweed is when you treat it, i.e. not suffering from drought or lack of water, the better the results will be.

Dormancy

Dormancy is the term given to the time when knotweed becomes inactive for a protracted period of time. It is a key part of the plant's annual cycle. Knotweed can also enter into an induced dormant state outside the winter period. The most likely reason for this phenomenon would be that the plant has been put under a level of stress that triggers it to shut down the production of surface growth, though activity in the rhizomes may still continue. Knotweed can remain dormant for a surprisingly long time, at least 20 years.

Herbicide treatment can induce dormancy. In the autumn, knotweed moves sucrose down from the leaves and stems into the rhizomes, via the crown, where it is stored during the winter. In the spring, when buds begin to form, if glyphosate herbicide has already been introduced during the previous growing season, the chemical will be moved with the sucrose as the plant grows. When transported to the buds, the glyphosate can weaken the emerging stems and either affect their formation – producing 'Bonsai growth' (see below) – or inhibit the growth completely, which will induce a period of dormancy.

'Bonsai' regrowth

Be aware that knotweed does not always look like knotweed. If it has been put under stress, knotweed can produce distorted, 'bonsai' regrowth (Figure 5.4). The distortion is typically caused by the application of glyphosate-based herbicides, or a severe dose of non-approved substances. Bonsai regrowth can take many forms.

Excavation

While herbicidal treatment will be the most commonly used method of remediating knotweed in domestic and commercial settings, there will be circumstances when full excavation of the knotweed

Figure 5.4 *Mild 'bonsai' regrowth typically contains smaller and elongated leaves, which are often wavy. Mild bonsai from crowns is usually quite stunted and bushy. The more extreme bonsai regrowth can take many forms and is often unrecognisable as knotweed by the uninitiated.*

will be required. There are many laws and practices that would need to be followed which will ensure the knotweed is removed and disposed of both efficiently and safely. It is highly recommended these works are carried out, or overseen, by a suitably qualified and experienced professional.

- Where knotweed has become established, excavating it without the use of a mechanical digger will be both impractical and dangerous.
- A newly established knotweed shoot, growing from a recently deposited, truncated section of rhizome, can be removed using a trowel.
- A small, immature infestation could be removed with a spade.
- All of the rhizome must be removed, otherwise knotweed will just grow back from the fragments that remain.

Figure 5.5 *Sometimes knotweed can be hand-dug, provided due care is taken not to leave any part of the plant in the ground. Here an immature knotweed plant was growing from a short, recently deposited fragment of rhizome.*

Removal

One of the key principles of knotweed excavation is to minimise knotweed as a waste product, and to question whether it needs to be removed from a site at all.

- Knotweed material is classified as a 'controlled waste' for which there are stringent procedures regarding its disposal.
- It must be disposed of at a licensed landfill site by prior arrangement (or possibly to a commercial incineration plant by special arrangement).
- Failure to dispose of it in this way can lead to criminal prosecution.
- Never place any viable knotweed material amongst your garden waste, or dispose of it at your local amenity tip.
- Landfill disposal (often known as 'dig and dump') is expensive; it is always better to deal with knotweed on site if at all possible.

The following activities may be encountered:

Burial involves burying the excavated knotweed on site in a 'burial cell' instead of removing it to landfill. Typically, this means the excavated knotweed material is fully encapsulated by a suitable root-barrier membrane. This method is really only practical on extensive development sites or large residential properties that have substantial areas of land within their boundaries, and would need to be carried out by contractors.

Bunding is a means of relocating knotweed to another area of the site where it can then be treated, but is only practical if there is available space.

Screening is a means of reducing the amount of excavated knotweed waste that needs to be taken off-site to landfill, but can never ensure soil is 'knotweed-free'.

The **_reduced dig_** involves excavation of the top half-metre of the soil, which contains the majority of the knotweed rhizomes and all the crowns. This would then be disposed of in the most appropriate way as the site allows (landfill, bunding, burial). The laying of a suitable membrane can be effective at containing the remaining rhizomes and preventing them from reaching the surface (Figure 5.6).

Root barriers

These are membranes used to limit and contain knotweed growth. They can prevent incursion from surrounding land, and be used to protect foundations or in the construction of burial cells. Other than for protecting structures, encapsulating or capping, the most common use for root barriers is along a boundary (Figure 5.7) where knotweed is present on adjacent land.

- Ensure the barrier is installed deeply enough (at least 2 to 3 m) to prevent rhizomes looping underneath it and growing up the other side.
- See that the barrier is long enough to prevent rhizomes spreading beyond it and growing around the edges.
- If you can get your neighbour to treat their knotweed, installing a root barrier would be purely for your peace of mind.

Figure 5.6 *A reduced-level excavation being horizontally capped with a root-barrier membrane to protect the foundations of a new footpath.*

Figure 5.7 *A root barrier membrane installed vertically along a boundary.*

Root barriers are only as effective as their quality. Do not cut corners when choosing one:

- Knotweed can push through cheap membranes (Figure 5.8) and standard plastic sheets;
- Membranes need to have a sufficient resistance to puncture and a minimum 50-year guarantee;
- Both porous and non-porous root barriers are available;
- When a membrane is installed horizontally, make sure it is porous enough to avoid possible flooding and will allow drainage;
- Disturbance of a root barrier by human or animal activity can render the barrier useless;
- Any damage to the membrane will simply be exploited by the knotweed.

Figure 5.8 A cheap or poorly-laid root barrier is no defence against knotweed.

Summary:

It is often appropriate to use different methods mentioned above on the same site, particularly if there are several areas of knotweed present.

It is important for householders to keep all documentation referring to treatment in a safe place. These would include:

- The original quotation or survey report, as these will establish the knotweed management plan;
- Records of site-visits and, if appropriate, the certificate of completion;
- If the property goes on the market, a future purchaser and related parties (e.g. solicitor, mortgage lender) will want to inspect this documentation.

Alternative methodologies

There will always be people who claim they have their own methods of dealing with knotweed. They say they will work just as well as the established methods, but at a minimal or no cost. Some suggestions reflect genuine environmental or safety concerns by avoiding the use of herbicides. However, these arguments can be undermined when the use of salt, oil, baking soda, washing-up liquid or some other substance is proposed (diesel, for instance!) that would prove to be much more damaging to the environment than an approved herbicide used in accordance with the recommendations on the label. The most common suggestions that do not involve damaging the environment are pulling, cutting, mowing, covering and burning.

Hand-pulling

Several sources recommend hand-pulling knotweed. This remedy is fine in itself but it is important to consider what is involved before embarking on it as your chosen method.

- The main advantage is not needing to apply any chemicals, making it ideal for use in areas of environmental sensitivity;

- Hand-pulling should only be considered for small infestations of knotweed, particularly those in their first year or two of growth;
- If the rhizome has spread more than a few centimetres, pulling will cause it to snap with some of it remaining in the earth;
- Pulling is extremely labour intensive;
- Both rhizome and crown material are likely to be extracted (Figure 5.9), so you will still have to face the requirements for disposal mentioned above.
- Even on small immature infestations you will need to allow several years (probably around three or more) of hand-pulling new shoots as they appear before you are likely to see a season without new growth;
- There is no guarantee of complete control, as remaining knotweed may have become so stressed that it retreats into dormancy for a while before returning at a later date.

Figure 5.9 Knotweed stems pulled during the winter whose crowns are still viable. Several active buds will continue to grow despite no longer being immersed in a soil medium.

Cutting

Cutting is a popular, but ultimately misguided, method of control. The theory is that by continually cutting the top growth you will weaken the root system to the point of death. Sadly, the more you cut knotweed, the more it will compensate by producing new shoots.

- Disposal can still present problems;
- Cut stems can be dried out and burnt if you have the facilities and within council byelaws;
- A prolonged period of cutting can eventually weaken the rhizome enough for it to stop producing new shoots, but this will take years;
- There is no guarantee that the rhizome will not simply revert to dormancy;
- If dormancy occurs, the knotweed will sit there for a few years until it is strong enough to start again.

Mowing

Mowing knotweed is similar to cutting and with similar drawbacks. The theory goes that mowing will eventually weaken the rhizome system and kill off the plant. However, this will take years to achieve with no guarantee that growth will not reappear once you stop mowing. Again, there is a disposal issue:

- New shoots can be highly regenerative, so you can't compost them with the grass.
- Mowing grass containing knotweed means that all your grass cuttings must then be regarded as knotweed waste;
- Separating the knotweed from the grass will be impossible;
- Wherever the mown cuttings go, you have created a high risk of spreading the plant to new areas.

Covering

Another popular method is to spread tarpaulins, membranes, or even carpets, over the knotweed to kill it by starving it of light and moisture. This is highly effective for some plants but not for knotweed, as the reserves to be found in the rhizomes are not readily depleted, even over extended periods of time.

If the covering is durable and strong enough to suppress the knotweed, it will have to be permanently in place, since knotweed can stay dormant but alive for a very long time. Once the covering is removed, the knotweed is likely to re-emerge.

Burning

Burning stems that have been cut down is a very effective means of removing the need to dispose of them off-site. Provided the stems have been cut above the first node and do not have any crown or rhizome material attached to them, they will burn easily, especially if they have been dried out for a couple of weeks or more. But be aware of the council byelaws regarding the burning of plant material.

Figure 5.10 A landowner tried burning his mature knotweed stand in situ. The resultant fire killed off the stems, but new growth emerged within a fortnight..

Burning the crowns and rhizomes is a more complex affair:

- Crowns in particular can withstand superficial burning;
- To truly kill off crowns and rhizomes requires temperatures of at least 45 degrees centigrade sustained throughout a period of over 48 hours;
- They can be burned effectively, but only if they are reintroduced to a bonfire many times until all that is left is ash;
- Do not try setting light to knotweed *in situ*; it will not kill the plant (Figure 5.10).

The consequences of knotweed disturbance

With knotweed's ability to regenerate growth from fragments of itself, any disturbance of the plant carries a level of risk. The following pictures show what happens if knotweed is mown, pulled, dug up, scraped or cut and not disposed of in a proper manner afterwards.

Figure 5.11 *Soil containing Japanese knotweed has been moved around on a site, resulting in new knotweed growth establishing in the soil stockpile.*

Figure 5.12 An amenity grass area has been mown, including the Japanese knotweed growing along the edges. The resultant distribution of knotweed fragments has led to new growth throughout.

Figure 5.13 A knotweed area has been cleared. The untouched rhizomes are already producing new shoots. The crowns (the dark areas) that have been left lying around are still viable.

45

Figure 5.14 *A JCB has scraped through a knotweed area and regrowth is starting to emerge (circled - see photo right for detail). Although not visible in the left-hand image, knotweed is also emerging in the piled earth at the end of the scraped area.*

Figure 5.15 *A combination of cutting and mowing has spread knotweed around this garden.*

Figure 5.16 *Several mature knotweed crowns have been disturbed. They are all viable, as evidenced by the bright orange rhizome material that has been exposed.*

Insurance-backed guarantees (IBG)

Mortgage lenders may refuse to lend to a buyer unless the property includes an IBG of knotweed management.

- The requirement for an IBG can come from mortgage lenders, developers, local authorities and various public bodies.
- While contractors can provide guarantees on their work, these guarantees can only be insured by a regulated insurance provider.
- To state an IBG is essential for the successful completion of knotweed remediation is untrue.
- An IBG is not a guarantee of successful eradication or control, and does not provide any protection against structural damage.
- It is also no guarantee of the quality of the work.
- An IBG is a guarantee that the work will be completed, and so just provides peace of mind.

- Insurance will only be offered by the insurer for knotweed works on the property owned by the client.
- While a contractor's guarantee may cover multiple properties, the insurance will only apply to one of those properties (unless the homeowner taking out the insurance owns more than one of them).
- If several properties are affected by the knotweed, any neighbouring homeowners requiring an IBG will have to take out a separate policy.
- Contractors should always make an IBG non-compulsory, and should not automatically include one in the cost of their remediation.
- A contractor should not sell an insurance product directly and should merely facilitate its implementation by acting as an intermediary between the client and the insurer.
- An IBG is not mandatory unless specified by, for example, a lender as a condition of a mortgage application.
- IBGs are only available for knotweed works and not for any other invasive plants (e.g. giant hogweed, bamboo, etc.).

Insurance cover

There will be some circumstances when an insurance-backed guarantee cannot be provided. Insurance products are offered entirely at the insurer's discretion and it is the insurer, not the contractor, who will decide whether the eligibility criteria have been met.

- An insurer can provide cover for completion for up to 10 years, some of which may involve monitoring beyond the finish of the actual remediating work.
- If, during the period of cover, the original contractor goes out of business, the insurance enables another suitably qualified and accredited contractor to be engaged by the insurer to complete the work.

- When remediation of knotweed has been completed and a separate monitoring programme is subsequently required, it is unlikely insurance will be provided for this new programme.

Contractors' obligations

- A contractor should itemise the price of the insurance or make it clear what the insurance product covers.
- Contractors are not allowed to charge more than a minimal administrative fee for recommending insurance, and should forward the insurer's own literature to the client to explain the product.
- If a contractor is directly selling insurance and is charging more than the stipulated administrative fee, this is fraudulent and should be reported to the Financial Conduct Authority.

Reinfestation

If there is a high risk of knotweed re-infestion of a site in the near future (e.g. if there is untreated knotweed on adjacent land), the insurance is likely to be refused by the insurer. Insurance can also be cancelled if the treatment programme is disrupted by unauthorised disturbance.

Finding impartial advice

Search the Internet and you'll find thousands of pages devoted to the subject of Japanese knotweed. How many of them can be trusted to tell you what you want to know? Who can you trust?

In 2012, the emergence of trade bodies created a greater level of regulation and conformity in the invasive weed industry, resulting in more confidence for clients. But it is still important to ask questions.

- Is the contractor a certified member of a trade body such as INNSA or the PCA?
- Qualifications and affiliations certainly help with the process of deciding on a contractor, but in themselves are no guarantee.

- Do contractors know what they are talking about; do they know the difference between 'control' and 'eradication'?
- Do they claim they can rid you of your knotweed in double-quick time?
- What herbicides are they proposing to use and how often? (Any more than two applications per year is highly suspect and is likely to exceed manufacturer's recommendations on dosage.)
- Does their guarantee give you what you require, or is it more form than substance?
- Does their period of guarantee involve annual site visits as a matter of course, or are they expecting you, the client, to inform them if the knotweed reappears?
- If the contractor is any good, their treatment programmes will stand up to scrutiny.

Amateur gardening websites and online forums can sometimes provide useful information – especially those that contain real-life experiences of treatments tried and results obtained – but exercise caution (see 'Alternative Methodologies' (p. 44)).

Trade bodies and other organisations

There are several organisations in the UK that can offer information and advice independent of any commercial agenda. They will not be able to deal with a situation for you, but they may be able to help separate fact from myth and point you in the right direction.

- The PCA (Property Care Association) formed its Invasive Weed Control Group (IWCG) in 2012 and now has a large membership. The PCA offers certificated training and created its own Knotweed Code of Practice in 2014.
- INNSA (Invasive Non-Native Specialists Association) is a contractor-led trade association. Formed in 2011, it drew up its own Knotweed Code of Practice in 2017.
- The Environment Agencies of the four home nations of the UK (EA. SEPA, NIEA, NRW)

regulate the management of knotweed waste, and ensure herbicides and other pollutants do not contaminate watercourses and drinking water. The Knotweed Code of Practice issued by the EA though withdrawn still offers some best-practice advice. There is no legal requirement to report the presence of knotweed to any of the agencies or Defra.

- Defra (Department for Environment, Food and Rural Affairs) is a UK ministerial, government department concerned with agriculture, horticulture, fisheries and a positive rural policy including wildlife conservation and biodiversity, along with protection of the environment and climate change, but It has no resources or remit to tackle knotweed on a practical level.

- The Non-Native Species Secretariat (NNSS) operates in conjunction with Defra and the various national governments to help co-ordinate an approach to tackling invasive non-native species in Great Britain; it published the *Great Britain Invasive Non-native Species Strategy* in 2008.

- The Japanese Knotweed Alliance is hosted by CABI (Centre for Agriculture and Bioscience International); it highlights the problems knotweed presents and promotes the concept of natural biological control.

- Local Authorities have no responsibility to manage knotweed growing on private property, though they do have a duty to deal with it on their own land if it is likely to encroach onto someone else's property or escape into the wild. Some of the more proactive local authorities have useful information about knotweed on their websites.

- The introduction of the Anti-Social Behaviour, Crime and Policing Act 2014 has enabled councils to become more involved in neighbours' disputes involving knotweed, but each council has taken its own view on how to apply this legislation.

Glossary of acronyms and common terms

Amenity: A feature of a property that increases its attractiveness and value to potential buyers or tenants. This can include location, proximity to shops, restaurants or schools, access to public transport, or road networks. A garden is also considered to be an amenity, and anything that restricts its use (e.g. Japanese knotweed) is said to have a detrimental impact on amenity land.

Annual: A plant that lives and dies in a single growing season. The plant will typically produce seeds or spores at the end of its life.

Anti-Social Behaviour, Crime and Policing Act 2014: UK legislation that extended nuisance laws. It can be implemented by either local authorities or the local police force, whereby Behaviour Orders or Protection Notices can be issued to someone deemed to have created a nuisance, and the Orders can be enforced if they are not complied with. While not specifically formulated for Japanese knotweed cases, the Home Office issued guidance in 2014 that suggested the Act could be used for this purpose.

BASIS: Originally an acronym, but now the trading name, of the organisation that trains practitioners and maintains high standards for the use and storage of agro- and environmental pesticides and herbicides. Contact details for BASIS can be found in the section below on Useful Telephone Numbers and E-mail addresses.

Biocontrol: The means of using a natural predator to control an invasive non-native species. The CABI has been trying to develop a biocontrol agent for use on Japanese knotweed since the early 2000s.

Bonsai: Stunted and distorted regrowth of Japanese knotweed, usually caused by previous herbicide applications. On rare occasions, it may be a symptom of a bacterial infection (*Candidatus Phytoplasma aurantifolia*).

Canes: Typically refers to the dead Japanese knotweed stems, which die back in the winter. The dead canes, if sufficiently mature, can persist upright for several years.

Crown: The dense, woody part of Japanese knotweed, which connects the underground rhizomes with the above-ground stems and from which buds will form. Crowns are evident in mature knotweed plants and are often partly visible above the surface. They can vary in size and shape, depending on the age of the plant and the growing conditions, and can have multiple stems emerging from them each season.

Defra: the lower-case acronym of the Department of Environment, Food and Rural Affairs, a Government department concerned with agriculture and horticulture, climate change, improving the health and diversity of the natural environment, the reduction of the global impact of the UK's food production and consumption, sustainable development and the rural economy.

EA: the Environment Agency in England concerned, in relation to knotweed, with licensing waste-management and landfill sites for disposal of controlled waste, and the protection of watercourses and drinking water from contamination by herbicides.

Dormancy: A period of inactive growth. Dormancy in knotweed can be partial or total, and can be long-lasting. Dormancy can be induced (for instance by treatment) or naturally occurring (triggered by unfavourable growing conditions, typically occurring every winter).

Efficacy: The effectiveness of a procedure or operation to control or limit growth.

Foliar application: Diluted herbicide applied to the leaves of a plant, typically by means of a spray.

Glyphosate: The active ingredient in many translocating, non-selective herbicides (e.g. Roundup).

Herbaceous: A plant whose stems are not woody, but are instead green and soft. The above-ground growth usually dies back during the winter but the plants may have underground parts that survive.

Herbicide: A type of pesticide used to control or kill plants, which can be residual, translocating, or both.

IBG: Insurance-backed guarantee, is a 'peace of mind' measure, often demanded by mortgage lenders. It is an insurance policy that protects the client's guarantee of treatment in the event that a contractor ceases to trade while working on a programme of knotweed control or eradication.

Inflorescence: A term used to describe the arrangement of flowers on a plant.

INNSA: Invasive Non-Native Specialists Association, a contractor-led trade body of knotweed specialists.

Internode: The section of hollow knotweed stem between two nodes.

Invasive non-native plant species: Plant species that do not occur naturally within the country in which they have been found. These plants (e.g. knotweed) have been introduced from other countries and their growing habits mean they have the ability to cause both ecological or economic damage to natural or semi-natural habitats.

IWCG: the Invasive Weed Control Group of the Property Care Association, formed in 2012.

JK or JKW: Most commonly used abbreviations for Japanese knotweed.

Monitoring: A series of observations over a set period of time.

NIEA: the Northern Ireland Environment Agency, formed in 2016.

NNSS: the Non-Native Species Secretariat. It published the *Great Britain Invasive Non-Native Species Strategy* last updated in 2015.

Node: The swollen horizontal ring around the Japanese knotweed stem from which leaves and lateral branches emerge. Each stem will be segmented by a number of nodes, dividing the stem into internodes.

NRW: Natural Resources Wales, the devolved Welsh Government's environmental agency, formed in 2013.

Panicle: A loose, branching cluster of flowers, where each branch contains more than one flower.

Pathway: A term used to describe the means of how an invasive non-native species is introduced onto, or spread around, a site.

PCA: the Property Care Association, which focuses on all aspects of the repair and protection of properties. It runs training workshops on dealing with invasive weeds such as knotweed, and has a wide membership of specialist contractors (and see IWCG above).

Perennation: The ability of an organism, such as a plant, to survive from year to year, especially when presented with unfavourable conditions between seasons (e.g. drought or winter). The parts of the plant that enable this survival are known as the **perennating parts**, which are typically storage organs (e.g. Japanese knotweed rhizomes and crowns).

Perennial: A plant that lives for longer than three growing seasons, continuing its growth from year to year (as opposed to an annual).

Pesticide: A chemical used to kill a pest. There are several groups of pesticides, such as: herbicides, fungicides and insecticides.

Propagule: Portion of a plant that, if separated from its parent, can grow into a new plant. Most typically rhizome and crown fragments in knotweed, but can also include seeds (where viable).

Remediation: The process of removing, or reducing the consequence of a problem that is having a detrimental effect on the environment. In knotweed terms, this is any programme or action of control or eradication.

Residual: Something that remains as a residue. A **residual herbicide** is one that remains active in the soil for a period of time following application.

Rhizome: A stem that grows underground, usually horizontally but can also angle down to depth. It acts as a storage organ for starches and proteins, which can be translocated along its length. It can produce buds or shoots and is capable of vegetative regeneration. Rhizomes last for more than one season.

Root: Part of the plant that absorbs water and nutrients from the soil and anchors the plant to the ground. They grow from the rhizomes and the crowns in knotweed.

Senescence: In biology, the term senescence refers to the process by which a cell ages and grows old. In plants, this can refer to the ageing or dying of a part or all of the organism. When referring to knotweed, the term represents the period when the leaves and stems age and die in response to harsher growing conditions, coinciding with the storage organs (crowns and rhizomes) drawing nutrients from the dying parts into themselves to overwinter.

SEPA: the Scottish Environmental Protection Agency, formed in 1996.

Species: A category of taxonomic classification, ranking below a genus or subgenus and consisting of related organisms capable of interbreeding.

Stand: A term used to describe a growth of plants in a particular area. It describes the visible area occupied by Japanese knotweed, particularly when mature and consisting of more than one individual plant.

Stem: The hollow, noded, above-ground part of knotweed plants, typically emerging from the crowns or the rhizomes, and which will have side stems or lateral branches and leaves attached.

Stem injection: A method of introducing precise amounts of herbicide into hollow stems. With knotweed, the stems are typically injected between the first and second nodes.

Sucrose: Plants naturally produce sugars, such as sucrose, glucose and fructose, as an end-product of photosynthesis. These sugars can be stored in leaves, seeds and roots of plants, providing energy for growth. Of the sugars, sucrose is more readily translocated within the plant, since it is more energy-efficient, both in its storage and in its transportation.

'The Wild': A location described in legislation (e.g. The Wildlife and Countryside Act 1981 (as amended), which makes it an offence to plant knotweed 'in the wild'). Defined by Defra as: 'The diverse range of natural and semi-natural habitats and their associated wild native flora and fauna in the rural and urban environments in general. This can also be broadly described as the general open environment.'

Translocation: The means of transporting absorbed substances within a plant. A **translocating herbicide** relies on this process to reach the roots of the target plant.

Trichome: A small hair or other outgrowth to be found on the surface of a plant.

Viable: Alive and capable of growth. Lack of visible above-ground growth is not a guarantee that a Japanese knotweed rhizome is unviable.

Weed wipe: A method of applying herbicide to leaves and stems, using a special weed-wiping device or a sponge soaked in herbicide (diluted in accordance with the label recommendations). A slower but more precise means of applying herbicide than spraying.

Source material

Books, guidance publications, codes of practice, reports

Lois Child & Max Wade, *The Japanese Knotweed Manual* (Packard Publishing, 2000).

Department for Environment, Food and Rural Affairs, *International Approaches to Japanese Knotweed in the Context of Property Sales* (Defra, 2020).

Environment Agency, *The Knotweed Code of Practice (Managing Japanese knotweed on development sites)* (Environment Agency, 2006).

Environment Agency, Your waste – Your responsibility. Frequently Asked Questions – version 2. Factsheet (Environment Agency - www.environment-agency.gov.uk).

Environment Agency, *Treatment of non-hazardous wastes for landfill: your waste – your responsibility.* Factsheet (Environment Agency, 2007 - www.environment-agency.gov.uk).

Invasive Non-Native Specialists Association, *Code of Practice: Managing Japanese Knotweed* (INNSA, 2017).

Non-Native Species Secretariat, *The Great Britain Invasive Non-native Species Strategy* (NNSS, 2015).

Property Care Association, *Code of Practice: Management of Japanese knotweed* (PCA, 2018 revision).

Property Care Association, *Japanese knotweed: Guidance for Professional Valuers and Surveyors* (PCA, 2022)

Royal Institution of Chartered Surveyors, *Japanese knotweed and residential property* (RICS, 2022)

Science and Technology Committee, *Japanese knotweed and the built environment* (UK Parliament, 2019).

Scottish Government, *Non-native species: code of practice.*
(Scottish Government, 2012

Stace, Clive, *New Flora of the British Isles. 4th edn* (C&M Floristics, 2019).

Websites

BASIS
(www.basis-reg.co.uk)

Cornwall County Council (knotweed pages)
(www.cornwall.gov.uk/environment-and-planning/
trees-hedges-and-woodland/invasive-plants/
japanese-knotweed/)

Department for Environment Food and Rural affairs (Defra)
(www.defra.gov.uk)

Environment Agency
(www.environment-agency.gov.uk)

GB Non-Native Species Secretariat
(www.nonnativespecies.org)

Japanese Knotweed Alliance
(www.cabi-bioscience.org/html/japanese_
knotweed_alliance.htm)

Natural Resources Wales
(www.naturalresources.wales)

Offwell Woodland and Wildlife Trust
(www.countrysideinfo.co.uk)

Pesticides Safety Directorate (PSD)
(www.pesticides.gov.uk)

Useful telephone numbers and e-mail addresses

Department of Agriculture, Environment and Rural Affairs (DAERA - Northern Ireland)
General enquiries: 0300 200 7852 (Monday to Friday, 9am-5pm)
Or e-mail: daera.helpline@daera-ni.gov.uk

Department for Environment Food and Rural Affairs (Defra)
General Enquiries: 03459 33 55 77 (Monday to Friday, 8.30am-5pm)
Or e-mail: defra.helpline@defra.gov.uk

Environment Agency (EA - England)
General enquiries: 03708 506 506 (Monday to Friday, 8am-6pm)
24-hour Incident Hotline: 0800 80 70 60
Or e-mail: enquiries@environment-agency.gov.uk

Natural Resources Wales (NRW - Wales)
General enquiries: 0300 065 3000 (Monday to Friday, 9am-5pm)
24-hour Incident Hotline: 0300 065 3000 (option 1)
Or e-mail: enquiries@naturalresourceswales.gov.uk

Northern Ireland Environment Agency (NIEA - Northern Ireland)
General enquiries: 0300 200 7856 (Monday to Friday, 9am-5pm)
Or e-mail: nieainfo@daera-ni.gov.uk

Scottish Environment Protection Agency (SEPA - Scotland)
At the time of writing (February 2022), SEPA had removed their telephone number and general enquiry e-mail address from their website due to the COVID-19 pandemic. However, they can be contacted through the online form on their website: www.sepa.org.uk/contact

Unless you are reporting something, before contacting any of the above you ought to check their websites (web addresses are provided in the previous section) to see if they have already published information to answer your query.

BASIS (Registration) Ltd:
Main Switchboard: 01335 343945
E-mail: help@basis-reg.co.uk
Website: www.basis-reg.com

Invasive Non-Native Specialists Association (INNSA)
General enquiries: 0800 1300 485
*There is no general enquiries e-mail address provided,
but queries can be directly e-mailed via the 'contact
us' page of their website: www.innsa.org*

Property Care Association (PCA):
General enquiries: 01480 400000
E-mail: pca@property-care.org
Website: www.property-care.org

If you are an amateur herbicide user looking for
general advice, it can be obtained from garden
centres and trade organisations such as BASIS
(above) and the Crop Protection Association
(website: www.cropprotection.org.uk)

About the author

Jim Glaister began working in the invasive weed sector in 2004, initially for Wreford Ltd until 2008, then freelancing for several invasive-weed companies. He joined The Knotweed Company in 2013. He attended the very first Certificated Surveyor in Japanese Knotweed (CSJK)  course run by the Property Care Association (PCA) and gained a Distinction in the exam when taken in 2014. He was subsequently given the PCA's Student of the Year award and was asked to join the roster of examiners and markers for the CSJK exam in 2015. He has continued in this position ever since, as well as contributing exam questions and developing the qualification and examination further.

He has been a contributing author to the Royal Institution of Chartered Surveyors' (RICS) online subscriber information portal *isurve* since 2009, providing the entries on Japanese knotweed and giant hogweed, and has delivered CPD presentations and webinars on a variety of invasive weed topics to environmental consultants, local authorities, property management companies and organisations such as RICS and the PCA. He is a member of the PCA's Invasive Weed Control Group and is on committees for developing educational courses and organising the PCA's annual invasive weed conference. He has been a Practising Associate Member of the Academy of Experts since 2020.

Jim is a co-author and editor of *Invasive Bamboos – their impact and management in Great Britain and Ireland*, published by Packard Publishing in 2021.

If you wish to contact Jim with new information, correct his mistakes or discuss any of the issues raised in this book, you can e-mail him at: jim@jkweed.co.uk